Palm Tree Bible Fun SEEK & FIND Book 1

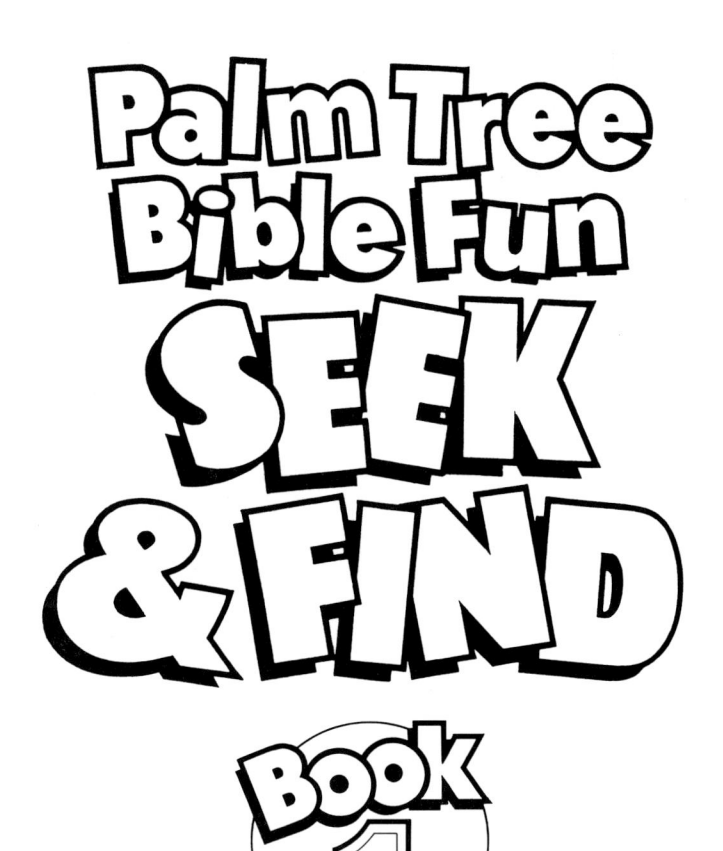

Illustrated by
Arthur Baker

Kevin Mayhew

Noah's Big Boat

Once, when the world was full of wicked people, God decided to send a great flood to destroy them all. But a farmer called Noah was a good man, so God told him to build a boat in which he and his family would be safe. He also told him to take with him two of every kind of animal.

When the boat was built, and Noah, his family and all the animals were on board, it started to rain. And it rained and rained until the whole earth was flooded. But Noah's boat sailed on for forty days until the rain stopped. Then Noah sent out a dove to find dry land, and when the dove came back with a fresh olive leaf in its beak, Noah knew that the floodwaters were going down.

At last the boat came to rest on dry ground and Noah, his family and all the animals came out to begin life all over again. Then God put a rainbow in the sky as a sign that there would never be another flood like that as long as the earth remained.

This story can be found in Genesis 6:5-9:17.

Things to Seek and Find

1. In picture 1, help Noah find his way to the good trees to build his boat.

2. Which animal has lost its mate? Which picture is it in?

3. How many differences can you find between the two Mrs Noahs in picture 6?

4. How many modern forms of transport can you find in the pictures?

3

4

5

6

Baby in a Basket

When the Hebrews were slaves in Egypt they had to make bricks to build Egyptian cities. But the Pharaoh thought there were too many slaves, so he ordered all Hebrew baby boys to be killed.

One Hebrew family hid their baby son by putting him in a basket among the reeds on the banks of the River Nile. When the Pharaoh's daughter came down to the river to bathe, she found the baby in the basket and wondered what to do with him. The baby's sister, who had been watching close by, came to the princess and said that her mother would be willing to look after him. The princess agreed. She called the baby Moses, and when he was old enough he went to live with her in her father's palace.

But when he grew to be a man, Moses was called by God to rescue the Hebrews from their slavery in Egypt.

This story can be found in Exodus, chapters 1 and 2.

Things to Seek and Find

1. How many Hebrew slaves are making bricks in picture 1?

2. How many differences can you find between the two Pharaohs in picture 2?

3. How many crocodiles can you see in the pictures?

4. In picture 3, help the princess to find her way to the baby in the basket.

4

5

6

7

Samson the Super Strong

Samson was famous for his strength. Once, when a young lion sprang at him, he killed it with his bare hands. He was always fighting against the Philistines, and once he caught some foxes, tied burning torches to their tails and sent them into the Philistines' harvest fields.

The Philistines thought they had caught Samson when he stayed in one of their towns, but Samson lifted the town gates off their hinges and got away.

The Philistines promised Samson's wife some money if she could find out the secret of his strength. When Samson told her that his strength lay in his long hair, she cut it off while he was asleep and the Philistines captured him.

While he was in prison, his hair grew long again and his strength returned. So when the Philistines took him to their temple for the crowd to jeer at him, Samson pulled down two great pillars and the temple collapsed on top of them all.

This story can be found in the Book of Judges 13:2-16:31.

Things to Seek and Find

1. In picture 4 help Samson find his way home through the cornfield where the Philistines are hiding.

2. How many differences can you find between the two running soldiers in picture 3?

3. How many daggers can you find in the pictures?

4. Can you spot ten things that don't belong in the pictures (apart from the daggers)?

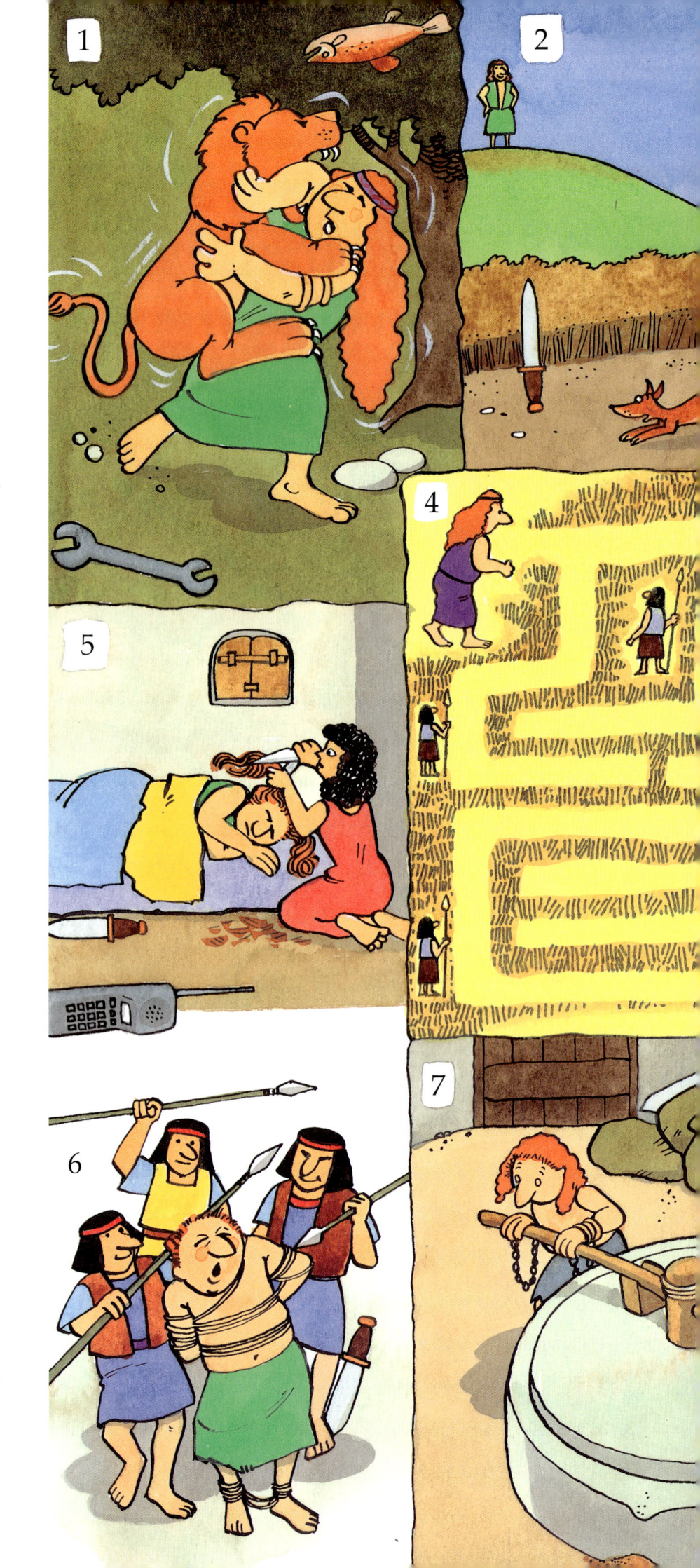

3

8

The Lost Son

Jesus told a story about a man who had two sons. The younger son, called Sam, asked his father for his share of the family money. Then he set off for the big city, where he soon wasted all his money enjoying himself at parties.

When he had spent his last penny and all his friends had left him, he got a job looking after pigs. But he was so hungry and miserable that he decided to go back home and tell his father how sorry he was for what he had done.

But when Sam's father saw him coming, he was so pleased that he rushed out to welcome him with open arms. And he ordered his servants to prepare a feast to celebrate his son's return.

But Sam's elder brother was jealous because Sam was being treated so well. So his father reminded him that *he* was loved too, and they should all be glad because Sam was back home again.

This story can be found in Luke 15:11-32.

Things to Seek and Find

1. How many differences can you find between the two brothers in picture 1?
2. Can you help Sam find his way back to his father in picture 6?
3. How many pigs can you find in these pictures?
4. At what time is the party taking place in picture 3?
5. What is the donkey called?
6. Can you spot eight things that don't belong in the pictures?

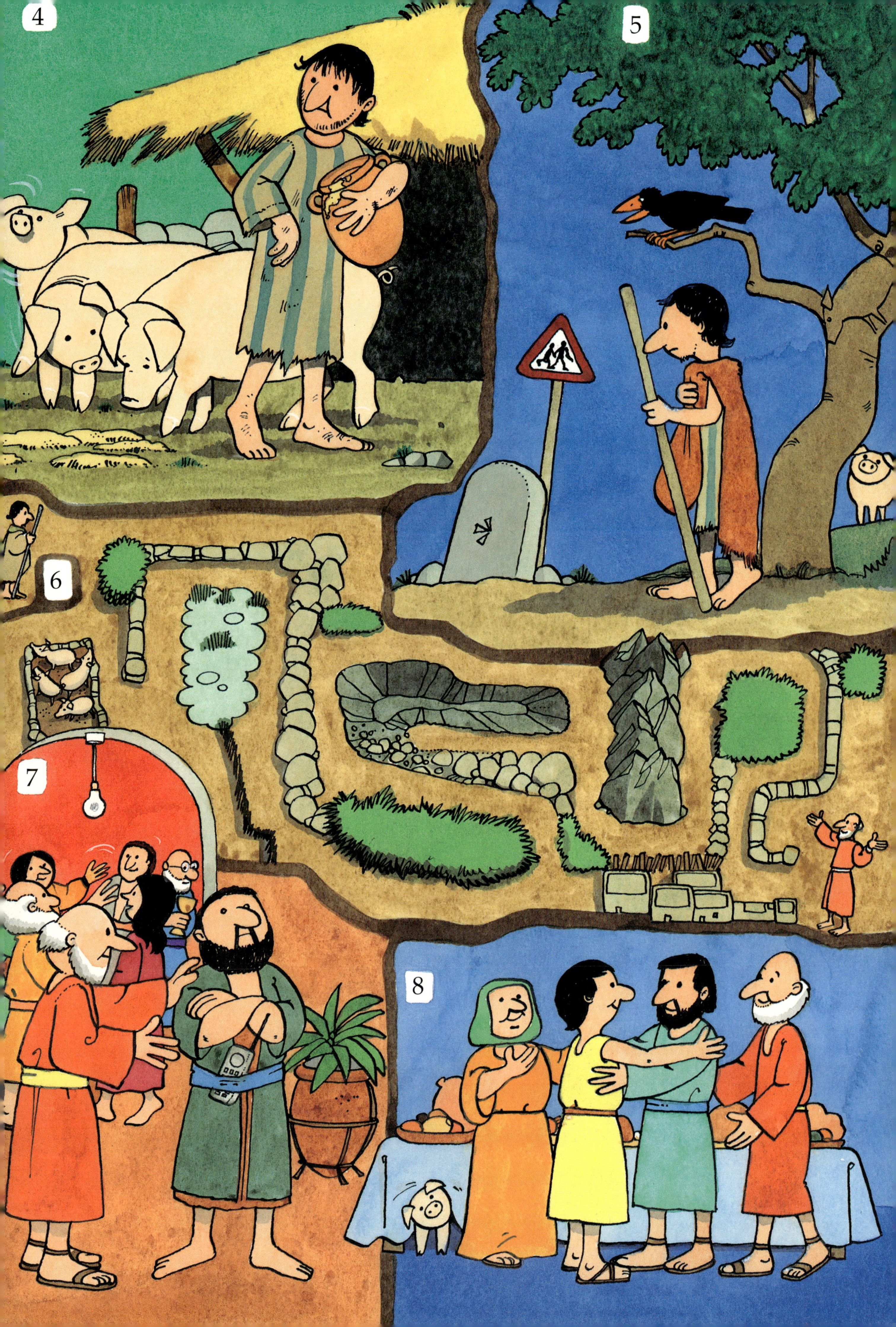
4
5
6
7
8

Jesus on the Sea

Jesus and his disciples were sailing across the Sea of Galilee, when suddenly there was a fierce storm and their boat was battered by the wind and waves. The disciples were terrified, but Jesus was sleeping peacefully in the stern. They woke him up and begged him to help them. So he stood up and ordered the storm to be still. And straightaway everything was calm. The disciples were amazed that the wind and the sea obeyed him.

Another time, Jesus was on the shore of the lake when he saw his disciples in their boat battling against a storm. He walked across the water towards them and when they saw him they were afraid. But Jesus said, 'Don't be afraid. It's only me.'

Then Peter wanted to walk on the water too, so Jesus told him to come to him. With his eyes on Jesus Peter stepped onto the sea, but when he saw the heaving waves he began to sink and cried out for help. Jesus grasped his hand and lifted him up and said, 'You need more faith.'

These stories can be found in Mark 4:35-41 and Matthew 14:22-33.

Things to Seek and Find

1. Can you help the fishing boat find its way to the fish in picture 2?

2. How many fish can you find in these pictures? (Watch out for the sharks!)

3. How many differences can you find between the two drawings of Jesus in picture 5?

4

5

6

7

8

Lionel the Lame Man

A lame man called Lionel, who lived in Capernaum, had heard that Jesus could make people well again. So when Jesus visited Capernaum, Lionel asked his friends to carry him to the house where Jesus was staying. But when they got there, they couldn't get in because there was a big crowd round the door.

Lionel's friends didn't give up. They carried him on to the flat roof, made a hole in it and lowered Lionel into the house, right at the feet of Jesus.

Jesus smiled at him and said, 'My son, your sins are forgiven.' Lionel felt warm inside when he heard that, and then Jesus told him to pick up his mat and walk home. To everyone's amazement that's just what Lionel did. His friends were delighted and said, 'We've never seen anything like this!'

This story can be found in Mark 2:1-12.

Things to Seek and Find

1. Help Lionel find his way to Jesus.

2. How many walking-sticks can you find in the pictures?

3. How many differences can you find between the two drawings of Lionel's friend waving to Jesus in picture 7?

4

5

6

7

Evil Beezil's Wicked Trick

Jesus told this story –

Jethro was a farmer, and he had a large field in which he sowed good seed. He was hoping to grow a fine crop of wheat. But one night, Jethro's bad neighbour, Evil Beezil, crept into the field and sowed weeds among the wheat.

When the weeds began to grow, Jethro's servants asked him if they should pull the weeds out in case they choked the wheat. But Jethro said, 'No. Leave them until the harvest. Then we will separate the weeds from the wheat and burn them.'

Jesus explained the story like this: 'I have called many people to follow me. They are like the good wheat seed that Jethro sowed in his field. But the devil has sent many bad people to turn the good people away from me. The bad people are like the weeds that Evil Beezil planted. At present the good and the bad are mixed up together. But the day will come when God will separate them. He will throw out the bad people and gather the good ones into his kingdom.'

This story can be found in Matthew 13:24-30 and 36-43.

Things to Seek and Find

1. Help Jethro (in picture 7) find his way to the field so that he can sow his seeds.

2. How many houses are there in the maze?

3. How many trowels can you find in the pictures?

4. How many differences are there between the two Jethros in picture 4?

Answers

Noah's Big Boat
Question 1. Find a way through the maze.
Question 2. The rabbit has lost its mate in picture 2.
Question 3. There are seven differences between the two Mrs. Noahs in picture 6.
Question 4. There are eight modern forms of transport: a helicopter, a balloon, a submarine, a car, a skateboard, a bike, a plane and a train.

Baby in a Basket
Question 1. There are sixteen Hebrew slaves making bricks.
Question 2. There are ten differences between the two Pharaohs in picture 2.
Question 3. There are eight crocodiles.
Question 4. Find a way through the maze.

Samson the Super Strong
Question 1. Find a way through the maze.
Question 2. There are seven differences between the two running soldiers.
Question 3. There are ten daggers in the pictures.
Question 4. The ten things that don't belong in the pictures are: an upside-down fish, a spanner, a boat, a tricycle, a telephone, a teapot, an aeroplane, a face at the window, a vacuum cleaner and a man with an umbrella.

The Lost Son
Question 1. There are ten differences between the two brothers in picture 1.
Question 2. Find a way through the maze.
Question 3. There are twelve pigs.
Question 4. The party is taking place at 3 o'clock.
Question 5. The donkey is called Ned.
Question 6. The eight things that don't belong in the pictures are: a flying pig, an electric guitar, a clock, a signpost, a light bulb, a pair of glasses, a telephone and a rubber tyre.

Jesus on the Sea
Question 1. Find a way through the maze.
Question 2. There are twenty-six fish. (Five are sharks!)
Question 3. There are six differences between the two drawings of Jesus.

Lionel the Lame Man
Question 1. Find a way through the maze.
Question 2. There are eight walking-sticks.
Question 3. There are eight differences between the two pictures of Lionel's friend.

Evil Beezil's Wicked Trick
Question 1. Find a way through the maze.
Question 2. There are nine houses.
Question 3. There are six trowels.
Question 4. There are six differences between the two pictures of Jethro.